If you were a SET

by Marcie Aboff

illustrated by Sarah Dillard

PICTURE WINDOW BOOKS
Minneapolis, Minnesota

set—a group that has something in common

Editor: Christianne Jones
Designer: Nathan Gassman
Page Production: Melissa Kes
The illustrations in this book were created with acrylics.

Picture Window Books
151 Good Counsel Drive
P.O. Box 669
Mankato, MN 56002-0669
877-845-8392
www.picturewindowbooks.com

Printed in the United States of America.

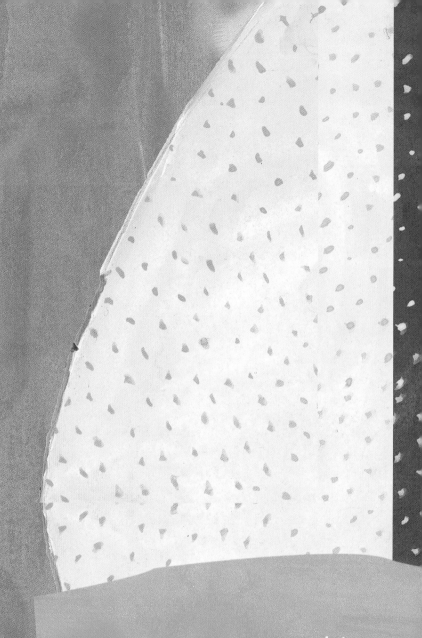

All books published by Picture Window Books
are manufactured with paper containing at least
10 percent post-consumer waste.

Library of Congress Cataloging-in-Publication Data
Aboff, Marcie.
If you were a set / by Marcie Aboff ; illustrated by Sarah Dillard.
p. cm. — (Math fun)
Includes index.
ISBN 978-1-4048-4799-6 (library binding)
ISBN 978-1-4048-4800-9 (paperback)
1. Set theory—Juvenile literature. I. Dillard, Sarah, 1961- ill.
II. Title.
QA248.A234 2009
511.3'22—dc22   2008006453

Special thanks to our adviser:
Stuart Farm, M.Ed., Mathematics Lecturer
University of North Dakota

If you were a set ...

... you could be a group of children, a group of *swings*, a group of *slides*, or a group of *dogs*.

4

5

If you were a set, you would be a group that has something in common. You could be sorted by color, size, shape, or some other feature.

Rudy's room was full of sets. He had sets of dirty clothes on the floor, a set of autographed baseballs on his shelf, and a set of sports trophies on his dresser.

If you were a set, you could be matched with objects in another set.

Mimi laid out a set of six colorful crayons.
Mo had a set of six pretty paints.
Mildred opened a set of six marvelous markers.

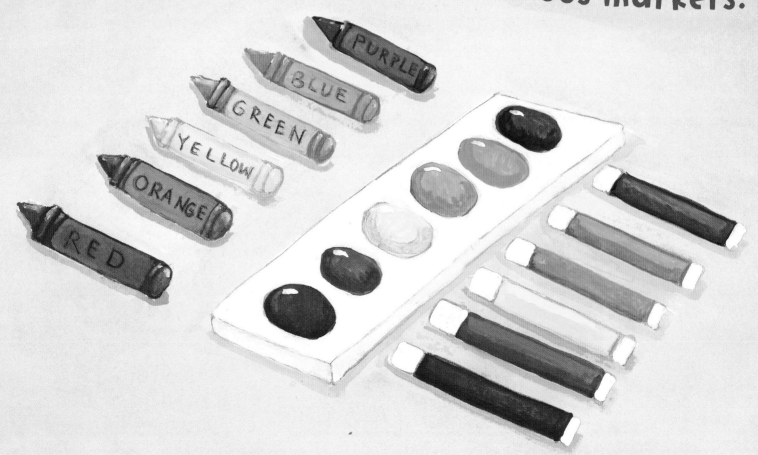

Together they created a masterpiece!

If you were a set, you could be arranged in different ways.

Lilly picked six peaches, two pineapples, and eight pears at the fruit stand.

She carried the fruits home, cleaned them, and created a fine fruit bowl with her set of fruits.

If you were a set, you could have a subset. A subset is a part of a whole set.

Billy loved books. He kept his set of books in a bookcase. There were picture books on the bottom shelf, chapter books on the middle shelf, and comic books on the top shelf.

All of Billy's books are a set of books. Three subsets are picture books, chapter books, and comic books.

If you were a set, you could take away a subset and still be a set. The remaining set would also be a subset.

Sally wanted to pack five pairs of shoes. But she could fit only two pairs of shoes in her suitcase. The two pairs are a subset.

Now Sally has a subset of three pairs of shoes left in her closet. Her set of five pairs of shoes is separated into two subsets.

15

If you were a set, you could be a combination of other sets.

Betty built a set of two yellow towers.

Bobby came to play and built
a set of three blue towers.

Billy came to play and built
a set of four green towers.

If you combine the three sets together,
you get one set of nine towers.

If you were a set, you could be compared to other sets.

Johnny picked a set of six roses, a set of four daisies, and a set of four petunias.

The set of roses was a larger set than either the set of daisies or the set of petunias.

The sets of daisies and petunias together was a larger set than the set of roses.

The sets of daisies and petunias had the same size.

18

Johnny combined the sets and gave
the beautiful bouquet to Josie.
She was overjoyed!

If you were a set, you would always know what belongs in your group.

Proper Pat had a perfect place setting of polka-dot dishes. Oh, no! One plate fell!

Pat had to use a plate from another set.
He was very upset that the plates were
not all the same.

You could be a group of singing sardines, swimming seals, or scary sharks ...

... if you were a set.

FUN WITH SETS

Sets are collections of things. Lots of people collect things such as toy cars, stuffed animals, stamps, and favorite books.

Make a collection of rocks. Start by collecting 10 rocks. Then sort them into subsets. Sort them by size, color, or shape.

Now make a collection of coins. Sort them by value (penny, nickel, dime, quarter). Then sort them by year.

What else can you collect?

Glossary

arrange—to place in an order

set—a group that has something in common

sort—to separate

subset—a set that is part of a larger set

To Learn More

More Books to Read

Aber, Linda Williams. *Grandma's Button Box.*
   New York: Kane Press, 2002.

Koomen, Michele. *Sets: Sorting into Groups.*
   Mankato, Minn.: Bridgestone Books, 2001.

Murphy, Stuart J. *Seaweed Soup.* New York:
   HarperCollins, 2001.

On the Web

FactHound offers a safe, fun way to find Web sites
related to topics in this book. All of the sites on
FactHound have been researched by our staff.

1. Visit *www.facthound.com*

2. Type in this special code: 1404847995

3. Click on the FETCH IT button.

Your trusty FactHound will fetch the best sites for you!

Index

sets
   arranged in different ways, 10-11
   as collections, 23
   combined, 16-17
   compared, 18-19
   definition, 6
   matching other objects, 8-9
subsets, 12-13, 14-15, 23

Look for all of the books in the Math Fun series:

If You Were a Fraction

If You Were a Minus Sign

If You Were a Plus Sign

If You Were a Set

If You Were an Even Number

If You Were an Odd Number

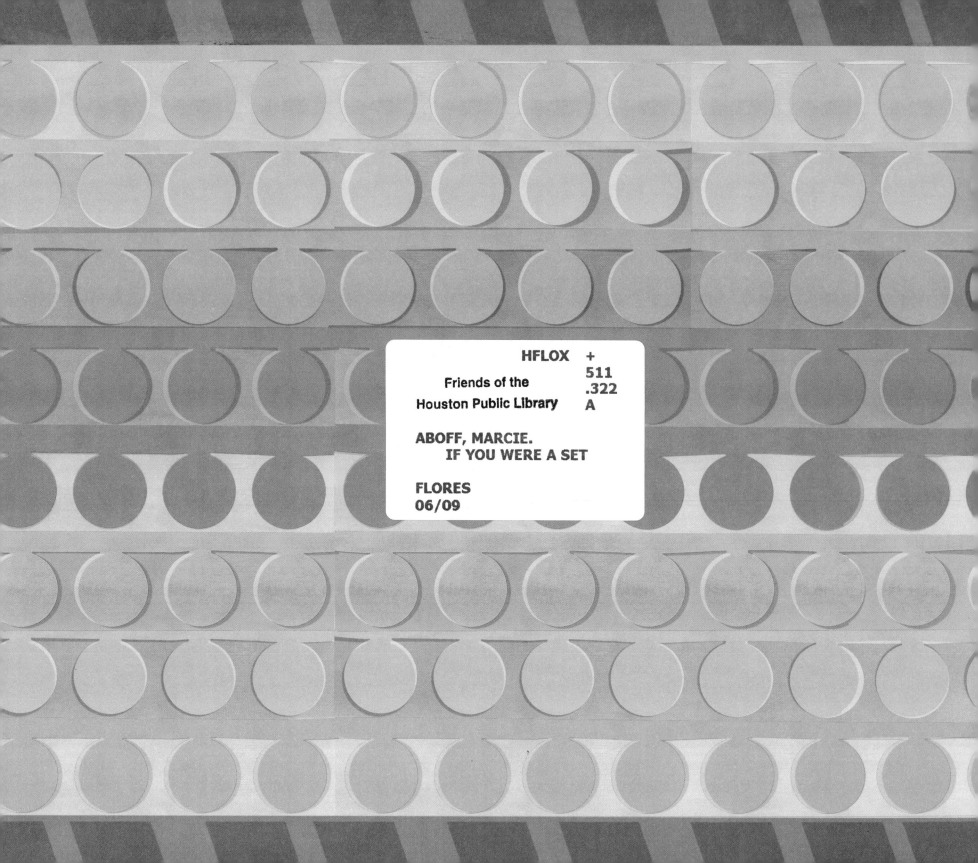